Baby Boomers - Recipes with Memories
Baby Boomer Recipes that Build Today's Culinary World

BY: Ida Smith

I0177092

License Notes

Table of Contents

Introduction

Baby Boomers' recipes are traditional recipes with so many stories streaming from them. These were the days of too many casseroles and creativity that packed a punch. In this recipe book, we will try to do justice to parents and grandparents that changed a generation. You may not like the foods, but you will eat them because of their stories.

The Best Mashed Potato

Usually served with gravy and a piece of chicken or beef, mash potatoes have come a long way. Over the decade, they have transformed variously, but we love this recipe.

Yield: 4

Total Prep Time: 35 minutes

Ingredient List:

- 900g Idaho potatoes peeled and cleaned
- ¼ cup unsalted butter
- 120g cream cheese
- 50g grated parmesan
- 1 cup milk
- 1 tsp white pepper

Preparation:

First, cook the Idaho potatoes in salted water until soft and almost breaking apart

Drain and break to pieces with a hand masher

Next, pour it into a mixer and add the rest of the ingredients

Whisk until smooth and creamy

Serve with gravy

The Classic Holiday Time Fruitcake

It was always a pleasure to finally bring the cake to the table during the holidays. Today, fruitcake is considered too busy and dense.

Yield: 6

Total Prep Time: 2 hours

Ingredient List:

- 1 cup glazed cherries diced
- 1 cup Medjool dates
- ¼ cup dried raisin
- ¼ cup dried prunes
- ¼ cup dried currants
- ½ cup candied pineapple
- ½ cup candied coconuts
- ½ cup chopped roasted walnuts
- 2 cups flour

- 1 tsp baking powder
- ½ tsp salt
- 1 full cup cream cheese
- 1/3 cup butter + 2 tbsp
- 1 cup sugar
- 3 large eggs

Preparation:
Add the whole fruits to a bowl and dust with 2 tbsp of flour
In a mixer, cream the cheese, butter, and eggs together
Add the sugar and mix until light, double in size, and super fluffy
Fold in the dry ingredients
Add the fruit mix, mix well and pour into a loaf pan
Bake low and slow until a skewer comes out clean

Budweiser Whole Chicken Roast

Budweiser was the beer of the days, and its rich, dark malty taste was better drunk or cooked with. It makes the best and juiciest chicken now.

Yield: 8

Total Prep Time: 2 hours

Ingredient List:

- 5 pounds whole chicken – giblets removed and cleaned
- 1 tall can Budweiser beer
- ¼ cup sweet chili sauce
- 1 tsp tamarind paste
- 1 tbsp onion paste
- 1 tsp ginger and garlic paste
- 1 tsp chili flakes
- 1 tbsp cane sugar ground
- 1 tsp cracked black pepper

- 2 tbsp chicken fat
- 2 tbsp unsalted butter
- Kosher salt
- 1 lemon cut in wedges

Preparation:
In a bowl, mix the entire ingredients together except the chicken, beer, and lemon

Dry the chicken with a towel

Press down to create space between the skins

Use the mixture to fill under the skin and rub the remaining all over the bird

Add some lemon wedges inside the and place the chicken on an opened beer can

Cook until brown and the dripping liquid is clear

Remove the can and serve as desired

Honey-Glazed Oven Roasted Root Veggies

They are better than canned vegetables and make a great side dish.

Yield: 4

Total Prep Time: 65 minutes

Ingredient List:

- 2 medium-sized sweet onions in wedges
- 2 cups sweet potatoes wedges
- 2 cups butternut squash wedges
- 2 cups parsnips wedges
- 3 cups baby carrots
- 1 cup baby beets wedges
- 1 tsp garlic powder
- 1 tsp paprika
- ¼ cup honey
- 1/3 cup olive oil

- ½ tsp black pepper
- Salt to taste

Preparation:
Mix the honey, oil, salt, and pepper in a cup
Add all the veggies in a bowl, pour the mixture over, and spread them evenly on a baking tray
Cover with foil sheet for the first 25 minutes and over for the next 30 minutes
Stir ad intervals to avoid burning them
Serve

Cottage Cheese Pancakes

The generation of today HATES cottage cheese. The lumpy mess is not appealing, but we have used it to create incredibly delicious and moist pancakes you will die for.

Yield: 4

Total Prep Time: 30 minutes

Ingredient List:

- ½ cup coconut milk
- ½ cup coconut cream
- 1 cup firm cottage cheese (squeeze out the excess liquid)
- 3 eggs
- 1 cup APF
- A dash of nutmeg
- A pinch of ground cloves
- 1 tsp cream of tartar

- ¼ cup caster sugar
- Margarine for the pan

Preparation:
Separate the egg into yolks and white
To the egg yolk, add the milk, cream, cheese and beat well
Add the dry ingredients – flour, sugar, nutmeg, and cloves into the wet mix
Beat the egg white with cream of tartar until stiff peaks are formed
Fold the egg white into the batter and allow it to rest for 10 minutes
Add margarine to a pan, pour a ladle of the mixture, and cook 2 minutes on each side
Flip when the edges start to bubble up
Serve as desire

Not Washington Watergate Salad

This classic dessert was eaten everywhere, from picnics to weddings and even at funerals. It uses simple ingredients to create amazing mouth-watering flavors.

Yield: 6

Total Prep Time: 10 minutes

Ingredient List:

- 1 box instant pistachio pudding
- 4 cups freshly cut pineapple chunks
- ½ cup pineapple juice
- ½ cup sweetened coconut flakes
- 2 cups mini marshmallows
- Maraschino cherries from garnish
- ½ cup toasted nuts of your choice

Preparation:

Whip everything in a large bowl together except for the cherries and nuts
Serve with a cherry and sprinkle of nuts

Homemade Fresh Corn Cornbread Muffin

During corn harvest, it was in abundance. Baby boomers had lots of ways to cook it, and this was one way.

Yield: 12

Total Prep Time: 20 minutes

Ingredient List:

- 1 cup self-raising flour
- 1 cup almond flour
- 1 cup yellow cornmeal
- 1 cup fresh corn from the cob
- 3 eggs
- 1 cup almond milk
- ½ cup sour cream
- ½ cup melted shortening
- ¾ cup caster sugar

Preparation:
Whisk the wet ingredients except for the eggs in a bowl
Add the dry ingredients and fold in well
Add the eggs and incorporate gently
Scoop into muffin papers and bake
Serve as desired

Moist Quick Nut Coconut Bread

The quick nut is a name every baby boomer will remember. We have tweaked this recipe and hope you love it.

Yield: a loaf

Total Prep Time: 70 minutes

Ingredient List:

- 2 cups bread flour
- 1 cup mashed ripe bananas
- 2 tsp baking powder
- 1 tbsp sugar
- 1 cup sweetened moist coconut flakes
- 300ml milk
- 2 tbsp vegetable shortening melted
- 1/8 tsp salt

Preparation:
Whisk the milk, banana, shortening, and coconut flakes in a bowl
Gradually add a mix of the flour, baking powder, sugar, and salt
Mix to form a moist dough
Pour into a loaf pan and bake until a skewer comes off clean
Cool on a rack and slice

Sweet, Spicy Ginger Bread Loaf

Nobody remembers this loaf because of the gingerbread man. It used to be a delicacy back in the days, and it was dark, rich, deep flavors that made an afternoon tea burst with deliciousness.

Yield: 8

Total Prep Time: 60 minutes

Ingredient List:

- 200ml coconut buttermilk
- 2 cups cake flour
- 2 large eggs
- 1 tsp baking soda
- ½ cup unsalted butter
- 50ml any soda of choice
- 1 tbsp ginger powder
- 1 tsp nutmeg powder

- ½ cup molasses
- ¼ cup black treacle
- ½ cup light brown sugar
- ½ tsp salt
- ½ tsp cloves

Preparation:
First, in a bowl, mix the dry ingredients and set aside
In the mixer, whisk the butter and sugar until the sugar is dissolved
Add the molasses, treacle, and eggs; beat again to incorporate
Next, add the soda to the buttermilk
Alternating between the dry and buttermilk
Add in the wet mixture until it is well- mixed
Then, spoon into a greased loaf tin. Bake
Cook and serve

2 Meats Meatloaf

It is certainly easier than making meatballs, and it is delicious. Having a slice of it on your plate with gravy and mashed potatoes is a perfect dinner.

Yield: 6

Total Prep Time: 70 minutes

Ingredient List:

- 350g lean ground beef
- 150g ground pork
- 1 cup bread crumbs
- 2 tbsp vegetable stock
- 1 tbsp brown sugar
- ½ cup chopped white onion
- ¼ cup mix of fresh parsley, oregano, and mint
- 1 tbsp soy sauce
- 1 tbsp Worcestershire sauce

- ½ cup ketchup
- 1 tbsp BBQ sauce
- Salt and pepper

Preparation:
First, combine the entire ingredients except for the BBQ sauce and ketchup
Scoop into a loaf tin and pat down
Next, bake uncovered for 45 minutes
Pour the BBQ and ketchup mix all over and bake covered
Serve

No more Condensed Soup Mushroom Chicken Soup

Condensed soup! Yuck, but no offense. Now, you can create this simple, delicious, heart-warming soup in minutes with canned ingredients.

Yield: 4

Total Prep Time: 25 minutes

Ingredient List:

- 1 cup shredded cooked chicken
- 2 cups chopped shitake mushroom
- ½ cup onion chopped
- 1 tbsp oil
- 1 cup heavy cream
- 700g chicken stock
- 1 tsp white pepper
- ½ tsp black pepper

- A handful of chives
 - Salt to taste

Preparation:
Sauté the onions in the oil until soft
Add the mushroom with half the stock and allow it to cook for 5 minutes on low heat
Add all the spices and cover
After 5 minutes, add the remaining stock, whisk in the heavy cream
Cook down some more
Add the chicken, taste for seasoning, and adjust accordingly
Serve with chives as garnish

Banana pudding on a stick

Give this baby boomer recipe an upgrade by making popsicles instead of a huge glass bowl. They are easier to eat, and kids love them.

Yield: 12

Total Prep Time: 30 minutes + freeze time

Ingredient List:

- 8 eggs yolks
- ¼ cup coconut flour
- 1 cup caster sugar – set aside 2 tbsp
- 750g full-cream milk
- 1 pack vanilla wafers
- 6 large ripe bananas cut
- 1 tsp banana essence
- A pinch of salt

Preparation:

Bring the milk, sugar, flour, and salt to a simmer

Meanwhile, beat the eggs yolks and pour some hot milk mixture while stirring

Return the egg yolk mixture to the saucepan and keep turning until it coats the back of a spoon

Allow it to cool down

Add the chopped bananas and crumble the wafers in the pudding

Pour into Popsicle tube and freeze

Halfway through, add the sticks and freeze until it is solid

Enjoy

Breakfast Sausages

Do you remember canned sausages in tomato sauce? They taste awful, but they made do. However, this is a great way to enjoy sausages.

Yield: 2

Total Prep Time: 40 minutes

Ingredient List:

- 1 cup seasoned panko crumbs
- 2 eggs
- 8 slices white bread
- 8 pieces your best sausage (chicken, beef, or pork)
- Oil for frying
- Salt and pepper

Preparation:

First, beat the eggs with salt and pepper in a bowl and set aside

In another bowl, pour the panko crumbs and add a little salt and pepper

Next, take the bread, roll it thin, place sausage and roll it up

Dip it in the egg mixture and then the panko crumbs

Then, fry with the seams down. Flip to cook the other side

Place on a kitchen towel and serve with ketchup or a dipping sauce of your choice

Bacon Crumbled Creamy Potato Salad

This showstopper will make any dinner tables envious. It is easy, and you can add whatever you like to it.

Yield: 6

Total Prep Time: 10 minutes

Ingredient List:

- 1 cup bacon crumbles
- 5 cups chopped cooked russet potatoes
- ½ cup caramelized onion
- 3 hardboiled eggs chopped
- ¼ cup celery
- 2 pickles chopped
- ½ cup mayo
- 1 tbsp yellow mustard
- ¼ cup unsweetened cream cheese

- Salt and pepper

Preparation:
Mix the mayo, cream cheese, mustard, and salt and pepper and set it aside
To the cooked potatoes, add the remaining ingredients and mix in with the mayo mix
Refrigerate and serve

Cereal Coated Oven Baked Chicken

Boy, there were lots of cereals back in the days. From the colorful round ones to the infamous Weetabix, the list is endless. Today, people are opting for a better and healthier breakfast option.

Total Prep Time: 70 minutes

Yield: 2

Ingredient List:

- 8 pieces soft chicken
- 1 tsp garlic powder
- 1 tsp onion powder
- 1 tsp chili flakes
- 1 tsp paprika
- 1 tsp dried thyme
- 1 tsp salt
- 1 tsp black pepper

- 1 cup buttermilk
- 1 egg
- 3 cups crushed cereal of choice

Preparation:
Season the chicken by massaging it into the flesh
Pour the buttermilk over and cover to sit for 15 minutes
Beat the egg in a bowl and pour the cereal into another bowl
Shake excess buttermilk of the chicken, dip in eggs, then in the cereal bowl, and place on a tray
Repeat for all and set into the oven
Serve as desired

Panko Crusted Creamy Mac & Cheese

Everyone loves mac and cheese, so do we? We have added a bit of pizzazz to make this more yum!

Yield: 4

Total Prep Time: 60 minutes

Ingredient List:

- 3 cups shell pasta cooked and drained
- 1 tsp paprika
- 1 tsp garlic and onion powder
- 2 cups smoked shredded chicken
- 1 tsp finely chopped red chili
- 2 eggs
- 2 cups shredded cheddar cheese
- 1 cup parmesan cheese
- 2 cups flour

- ¼ cup butter
- Salt and pepper
- 1.5 cups panko crumbs

Preparation:
First, in a large bowl, whisk the flour, egg, cheeses, salt and pepper, paprika, chili, and onion powder

Add the chicken shreds and macaroni and stir well

Taste for seasoning and adjust according

Next, pour into a casserole dish and pat down

Mix the crumbs and butter

Then, layer it all over the dish and bake for 45 minutes on high

Reduce for 10 minutes and serve after cooling down

Honey Lime Fresh Fruit Cocktail

It used to be out of a can. The fruits would be soggy, but it had to be eaten. This fresh cocktail is healthy and delicious.

Yield: 4

Total Prep Time: 10 minutes

Ingredient List:

- 1 cup strawberries chopped
- 1 cup green apple chopped
- 1 cup blackberries
- 1 cup raspberries
- 1 cup golden melon chopped
- 1 cup watermelon chopped
- 1 cup pineapple chopped
- 1 cup red grape sliced
- 1 pomegranate seeds

- 12 mint leaves
- ½ cup honey
- 1 tsp lime juice

Preparation:
First, finely chop half of the mint leaves and simmer in honey and lime juice
Add all the fruits into a large bowl
Then, pour over the honey-mint-lime mix
Toss, chill and serve when ready

Fresh fillets Fish Sticks

Oh, the good old days, fish sticks. Now we have access to fillets and can make them at home.

Yield: 4

Total Prep Time: 30 minutes

Ingredient List:

- 4 fish fillets cut into strips
- 1 tsp paprika
- 1 tsp cayenne
- Salt
- 2 cups cornstarch
- Oil for frying

Preparation:

Season the fish fillets

Coat in cornflour and shake off any excess
Fry until brown and crunchy

Biscuits made with Margarine

Today, margarine is deemed unhealthy because of the fat content. Yesterday, it was the best ingredient in a boomer kitchen. You know everything tastes good with margarine.

Yield: a lot

Total Prep Time: 30 minutes

Ingredient List:

- 3 cups self-raising flour
- 4 large eggs
- ½ cup coconut flour
- ½ cup brown sugar
- ¼ cup white sugar
- 1 tsp vanilla extract
- 1 tsp lemon juice
- 250g margarine choose the best in your area

Preparation:
Beat the eggs, sugars, lemon juice, and vanilla extract in a mixer
Add the flour and whisk in
Gradually add the melted margarine until a smooth dough is formed
Cut to the desired shape and bake until brown

Lemon Cake Snack Cakes

Snack cakes use to treat every baby boomer cupboard. These treats will spend forever and never get spoilt. Wonder how they make them those days; this is our take on it.

Yield: 12

Total Prep Time: 40 minutes

Ingredient List:

- 1 box lemon cake mix
- 1 egg white
- 2 cups icing sugar
- 1 tbsp milk
- 1 tsp vanilla extract

Preparation:

Mix the cake mix according to the packet instructions

Pour the batter into a square tin and bake
Meanwhile, whisk the egg white until frothy
Add the icing sugar until a spreadable consistency is obtained
If it is too thick, loosen with water or leave it out
Mix in the vanilla and pour over the cake when it is cooled

No More Canned Pasta

It used to be canned pasta in tomato sauce, but this recipe is so easy to make and tastes better.

Yield: 6
Total Prep Time: 30 minutes
Ingredient List:

- 3 cups APF
- 5 eggs
- 1 tsp ginger powder

Preparation:
Add everything to a mixer and combine until it does not stick to the sides
Wrap in a cling film and rest for 5 minutes
Remove and roll out as thin as possible
Cut to the desired shape

Cook immediately

Ginger Flavored Blue Cheese Dip

Definitely not for faintheartedness, blue cheese is on another level. Most people do not like the pungent and tangy taste, but they make some for the best dip.

Yield: a bowl

Total Prep Time: 5 minutes

Ingredient List:

- 1 cup blue cheese
- ½ cup heavy cream
- ¼ cup mayo
- 1 kefir lime
- 1 tsp minced ginger
- 1 tsp sugar
- A pinch of salt
- ½ tsp cracked black pepper

Preparation:
In a bowl, mix the entire ingredients except the pepper
Sprinkle the pepper just before service but refrigerate after it is made

Easy Tuna Salad

Definitely take the salt taste out of canned tuna. It is simple and tasty and pairs well with anything.

Yield: 2

Total Prep Time: 15 minutes

Ingredient List:

- 1 cup shredded tuna
- 1 small shallot chopped
- 6 cherry tomatoes diced
- 1 cup cucumber seeded diced
- 1 cup black olives diced
- 300g lettuce
- 1 tsp warm honey
- 2 tsp lemon juice

Preparation:
Mix the honey and lemon juice together
Add everything to a bowl
Drizzle the honey mix and serve

Spam Spamming Fried Rice

The popular meat of World War II become so on-demand because of how easy it is to use. You would always find one in a boomer home.

Yield: 4

Total Prep Time: 40 minutes

Ingredient List:

- 1 cup sweet corn
- 1 tsp red chili chopped
- 1 small onion chopped
- 1 red and yellow bell pepper diced
- 2 tbsp diced leeks
- 3 tbsp carrots diced
- 2 tbsp peas
- 4 cups cooked rice
- 1 can spam, diced into bits

- 1 tsp garlic minced
- ½ tsp ginger minced
- 1 tbsp oil
- 1 tbsp butter
- Salt and pepper

Preparation:
First, add the oil and butter to a pan
Sauté the onion, leeks, garlic, ginger, and chili for a minutes
Add the carrots, peppers, and spam, cook until spam has some crust to it
Next, add the rice and stir well
Season and add the corn
Serve

Super Healthy Mayonnaise recipe

Mayo was almost on every dish back in the days. At this time, we have made it healthier and more delicious than old ones.

Yield: a jar

Total Prep Time: 10 minutes

Ingredient List:

- 2 eggs
- 1 tbsp lemon juice
- 1 tsp yellow mustard
- 1 tsp chili paste
- 1 tsp honey
- 1 tsp salt
- 500g avocado oil

Preparation:

Add all the ingredients to a blender
Gradually add the oil as it whizzes until it emulsifies
Scoop in a bowl

Not McDonald's Burger Patties

Those were the days of McDonald's, the family would drive there just to have a burger, and the patties were so juicy.

Yield: 6

Total Prep Time: 30 minutes

Ingredient List:

- 2 pounds ground beef
- 1 pound ground pork lean
- 1 tsp black pepper
- 1 tsp minced garlic
- ½ tsp chili chopped
- 1 tsp mixed dried herbs
- 2 shallots finely chopped
- 1 egg
- 1 tbsp soy sauce

- 1 stick butter
- Kosher salt to taste

Preparation:
Melt a tbsp of butter in a pan
Sauté the onion, garlic, and chili with a pinch of salt and pepper
Allow it to cool down
Meanwhile, add the ground meat in a bowl, pour the onion mix, add the eggs, soy, and herbs
Mix gently and season with the salt and pepper
Make the patties to the desired size and line them up on a baking tray
Take small chunks of butter and insert it into the patties
Use when ready, and they freeze well too

Deep Fried Beef Liver

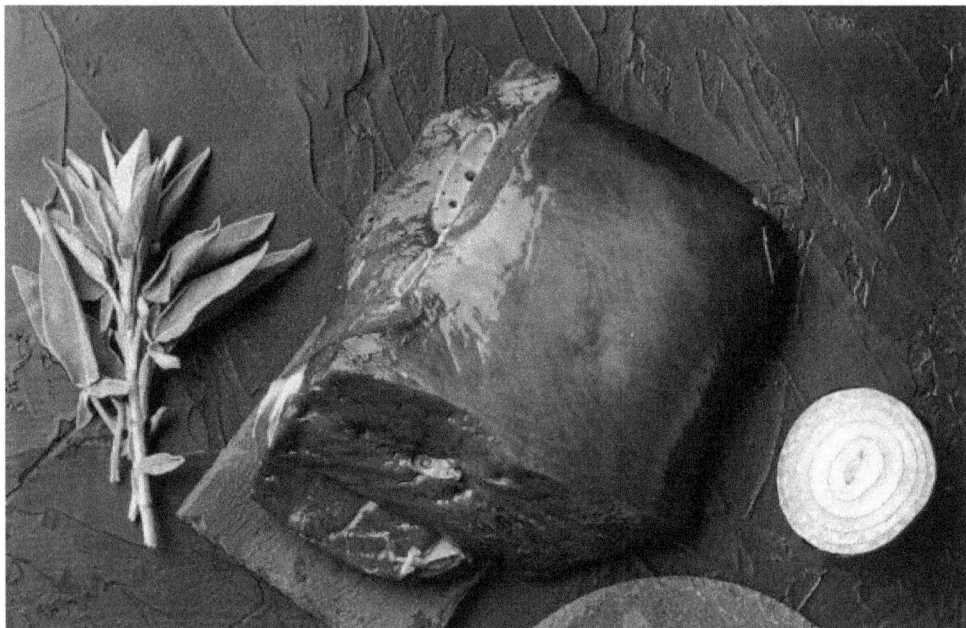

The liver was never a likable dish back in the days and still is not today. It tastes great, and a good way to eat it is to fry livers crisp.

Yield: 1

Total Prep Time: 30 minutes

Ingredient List:

- 2 thinly sliced beef livers
- ¼ cup soy
- 1 garlic clove
- 1 tsp ginger
- 1 red chili
- 1 cup cornflour
- Oil for frying

Preparation:

Blend the soy, garlic, ginger, chili to a paste

Pour the paste all over the liver and marinate for 5 minutes
Remove, coat with flour, and fry
Serve

Repurpose Baked Bean for Breakfast

Along came frozen food, canned food, and TV dinners, and this is one of them. We are tweaking the famous baked beans for breakfast.

Yield: 2

Total Prep Time: 15 minutes

Ingredient List:

- 1 can baked beans in tomato sauce
- 4 eggs
- 1 tsp olive oil
- 1 small shallot chopped
- 1 tbsp chopped cilantro
- ½ tsp black pepper

Preparation:

Sauté the shallot in the oil until soft

Add the baked beans and cook until reduced
Crack the eggs in the pan at a different point
Reduce the heat and cover to cook
Sprinkle with black pepper and serve with toast.

Almond Coconut Macaroon

These were very popular in Jewish-American homes and were made during the holidays. They were a treat then and still are today.

Yield: a lot

Total Prep Time: 30 minutes

Ingredient List:

- ½ cup sugar
- 4 cups sweetened coconut shreds
- ¾ cup almond flour
- 4 egg whites
- 1 tsp lime zest
- ½ tsp coconut essence
- ½ tsp vanilla essence

Preparation:

First, beat the egg whites and sugar until soft peaks are formed

Fold in the coconut, almond flour, lime zest, and essence to make a batter
Next, using a largemouth piping bag
Pipe the mixture on a lined baking tray
Then, bake until it is set and firm
Cool and store

Fountain chocolate drink

This is a fizzy creamy drink with all the flavors you love.

Yield: a glass

Total Prep Time: 5 minutes

Ingredient List:

- ¼ cup full-fat cream milk
- 4 tbsp thick dark chocolate syrup
- ½ cup seltzer
- A dash of vanilla

Preparation:

Add the milk, vanilla, and chocolate syrup to the glass

Gradually pour the seltzer water to fill and stir

Enjoy immediately

Conclusion

You may not like everything that was cooked, but you cannot deny the fact that going to grandma's house was because of the food. They were rich and super flavorful.

If you are looking to add some traditional spice and flair to your modern cooking, dig out your mom's and grandma's recipe book. It will be a journey. In the meantime, the 30 recipes should get you started.

Don't miss out!

Visit the website below and you can sign up to receive emails whenever Ida Smith publishes a new book. There's no charge and no obligation.

https://books2read.com/r/B-A-LRXL-CWVJB

BOOKS 2 READ

Connecting independent readers to independent writers.